PRESSURE SYSTEM
Instructor Edition

PRESSURE SYSTEM
A Field Manual for Paradox
Instructor Edition
J. A. Gucci

PRESSURE SYSTEM
Instructor Edition
© 2026 J. A. Gucci
All rights reserved.

No part of this book may be reproduced, stored in a retrieval system, or transmitted in any form or by any means—electronic, mechanical, photocopying, recording, or otherwise—without prior written permission of the author, except for brief quotations used in reviews or scholarly discussion.

This book is a work of poetry. Any resemblance to actual persons, living or dead, or actual events is incidental and unintentional.

First edition

ISBN: 979-8-9946751-1-3

Printed in the United States of America

CONTENTS

I. CONDITIONS

Hayflick
Umfeld
Cracked Shells
Ballast
Still Dangling
Kettle Lake
Snow Sheath
Playa Bloom
June Gloom
Zero Shadow Day
Iteration
Ironwood
Boom
Bread
Lee Side

II. TENSIONS

Lydian
Dotted Line
Laid Out
Long Roll
Holdfasts
Crystallography
Camera Click
Callus

Road Rash
White Smoke
Tessellation
Tavy
Infinity
Qualia
Chilling Hour
Gazpacho

III. ECHOES

Residue
Ghost Perch
Koala Plate
Chef's Kiss
Gaze
Antiseptic
Epoxy
Panhandle Hook
Box Jelly
Tennis Court

Preface

Pressure System is not a collection of metaphors. It is a collection of mechanisms—each poem shaped by observable systems under stress.

Across biology, physics, weather, and emotion, the poems follow a triadic loop: compression, break, release. The structure is consistent, but what it reveals is not. Each system behaves according to its own materials and limits—some fracture, some adapt, some transform entirely.

This book is designed for students who are learning to write with precision rather than sentiment. It teaches them to locate tension in the physical world, and to translate that tension into form. The goal is not symbolic interpretation, but structural recognition. What is the source of pressure? Where does the break occur? What's left behind?

These poems do not stand for something else. They are what they show. The students' task is to observe, and then to build—sentence by sentence—a pressure system of their own.

To the Instructor

This edition of Pressure System is built for classroom adoption across writing, literature, and interdisciplinary courses. Whether you're teaching creative writing, poetics, or composition, the book provides a scaffolded approach to systems-based thinking and poetic construction.

Each entry in the standard edition is accompanied here by:

- A **Paradox Triad** — three interrelated concepts that shape the tension in the poem

- **Scientific or Structural Context** — real-world mechanisms (ecological, physical, biological) that mirror the emotional architecture

- **Discussion Prompts** — open-ended questions to generate observation, analysis, and revision

- Creative Response Ideas — writing experiments and scaffolded generative exercises

- **Command Line** — a single imperative that distills the paradox into action

You may teach from Pressure System in sequence or by emotional grouping (e.g., "states of containment," "threshold events," "trauma and aftershock"). The entries build understanding cumulatively, but each poem is also self-contained. Students need not decode the poem to understand it—they must observe its behavior.

This edition encourages cross-disciplinary teaching. Instructors from biology, physics, or environmental science may find surprising parallels to core concepts in their own fields. The book rewards collaboration.

There is no "key" or answer sheet. The poems operate like systems: pressure builds, something breaks, and something remains. Your students' job is to trace that movement—with precision, empathy, and care.

How to Use This Book in Class

Pressure System is designed as a modular teaching text. Each poem operates within a compressed structure—a pressure system—centered around a paradox triad. This allows instructors to approach the material from multiple pedagogical angles: emotional, scientific, linguistic, or compositional.

Suggested Approaches

1. Close Reading by Compression

- Begin by reading the poem aloud.
- Identify the nouns, verbs, and physical phenomena.
- Ask students: Where does pressure build? Where does release happen?
- Discuss the Command: What kind of behavior is it modeling or resisting?

2. Triad-Driven Analysis

- Introduce the triad before showing the poem.
- Have students guess what kinds of systems or behaviors might arise from those terms.
- After reading, map the poem back to the triad to reveal hidden architecture.

3. Science + Emotion Integration

- Use the Scientific Context section to ground the poem in real-world phenomena.
- Pair poems with short science readings or videos.

- Discuss: What does this system explain emotionally that it also explains physically?

4. Creative Emulation

- Assign students to write their own pressure system poems using a given triad.
- Use the Creative Response prompts as scaffolding.
- Emphasize that poems do not have to be metaphorical—they can be observational systems.

5. Collaborative Mapping

- Build a wall chart of all triads and link them with string or color to track evolving themes (e.g., containment, rupture, adaptation).
- Assign groups to "adopt" a poem for deeper study and presentation.

What Is a Pressure System?

A **pressure system** is a structure—emotional, physical, or poetic—in which opposing forces build, distort, and resolve. In this book, each poem is built on a **paradox triad**: three words in tension that form a loop. These triads are not abstract metaphors. They are observable systems pulled from the physical world—things that crack, fuse, seethe, balance, rupture, or converge.

Each entry asks:
What happens when internal pressure mirrors external structure?
What kind of poem forms when language is treated like physics?

A pressure system poem:

- Compresses emotion without declaring it.
- Draws from biology, geology, mechanics, and weather.
- Anchors abstract experience in observable process.
- Substitutes metaphor with friction, force, and constraint.

The goal is not to explain feelings.
The goal is to **engineer** them.
A pressure system doesn't describe pain—it enacts it.

It doesn't describe wonder—it builds a chamber for it.

By pairing scientific fact with emotional resonance, these poems invite interpretation that is **structural, not symbolic.** They require readers—and students—not to guess what something "means," but to observe how it **works.**

About the Triads

Each poem in Pressure System is built on a **paradox triad:** three words locked in tension. These are not steps in a sequence. They do not represent beginning, middle, and end. Instead, they form a **loop**—a self-contained system in which energy, conflict, or transformation cycles indefinitely.

Each triad is:

- **Concrete** — no abstractions.
- **Contradictory** — each element resists the others.
- **Charged** — together, they create a system of pressure and release.

Example triad:

Crack / Ice / Water
Each word implies change, collapse, or flux. No one element is dominant, and none can be fully understood without the others. Together, they form a poetic engine.

Each triad in this collection:

- Informs the poem's structure.
- Shapes its emotional trajectory.
- Mirrors physical processes found in nature or science.

By organizing poems around these triads, Pressure System offers a repeatable, scalable method for teaching poetics rooted in **constraint, precision, and design thinking.** Students are not asked to write "about" a feeling. They are taught to **build a system** that **produces** it.

How to Use This Book in the Classroom

Pressure System is designed for high school classrooms but is flexible enough to adapt to a range of grade levels, from middle school through early college. Each poem, triad, and activity is structured to foster **close observation, creative risk, and systems thinking**. Here's how you can bring it into your classroom:

1. One Poem at a Time

Start class with a single poem. Read it aloud. Project it on the board. Ask students:

- What is happening, literally?
- What might the triad be? (If not already given)
- What is the loop? What returns?

Encourage students to observe before interpreting.

2. Triad Analysis

Each triad operates like a pressure system—pushing against itself, generating poetic energy. Guide students to:

- Identify each word's function (static, dynamic, hinge?)
- Explore how the words interact
- Map the triad to scientific or emotional processes

This supports both analytical and creative thinking.

3. Loop Writing Prompts

Invite students to create their own triads:

- Concrete Noun / Opposing Noun / Collision or Outcome
  Then, write a short poem constrained by that triad. Emphasize:
- No metaphors
- No explanations
- Compression and image

This builds poetic fluency while training design-based composition.

4. Command Lines

Each poem concludes with a "Command" — a distilled imperative derived from the poem's logic. These are not morals or takeaways. They are compressions:

- Invite students to write their own commands after reading
- Use them as entry points for class discussion or journaling

5. Cross-Disciplinary Connections

Many poems are rooted in physics, biology, geology, or weather systems. Partner with STEM educators to:

- Explore the scientific principles behind each triad
- Conduct micro-research to support writing
- Create science/poetry collaborative projects

6. Assessment & Portfolios

Student progress can be measured by:

- Quality and originality of triads
- Clarity and compression in poems
- Ability to identify and explain poetic loops
- Final portfolios showing growth across poems, revisions, and command lines

This book is less about interpretation, more about engineering emotion through form and precision. It teaches students how to build meaning without sentimentality—and how to write with constraint without sacrificing voice.

What Is a Loop Poem?

Loop poems are short, image-based poems built around a triad—three linked concepts that orbit or collide to create tension, transformation, or paradox. These poems are not metaphorical. They are observational, structural, and precise. The loop is what returns—either in language, logic, image, or rhythm.

Key Features:

- **Compression**: Every word is necessary. Articles and explanations are stripped away.

- **Image over Metaphor:** Poets describe what is seen, heard, or measured—not what something "means."

- **Tension-Pressure-Release**: The form often follows this rhythm. A setup, a disruption, and a residue.

- **Command Line**: Each poem ends with a distilled imperative—compressing the triad into an emotional or behavioral principle.

Why "Loop"?

Loops show **systems** in motion:

- Water to vapor to rain
- Heat to pressure to explosion

- A mistake to a memory to a pattern

Poems don't need to explain the loop. They just need to **embody** it.

What Makes It Work?

The Triad. Every poem in Pressure System is rooted in a triad—often:

- A condition / a force / a transformation
- A state / an interruption / a return
- A pressure / a break / a bloom

By focusing on what is observable and structural, students learn how to **build emotion from form**, not just from feelings.

On Commands and Compression

Each poem in Pressure System ends with a **Command Line**. These lines are not morals, morals, or mantras. They are **distillations**—what remains after pressure has been applied.

What Commands Do

- **They transform the poem into action.**
- **They shift attention to the reader.**
- **They compress the poem's logic into a single behavioral gesture.**

Commands do not explain the poem. They extend it—into risk, decision, or change.

Example

Poem: A glass pane shatters—still hanging.
Command: Leave it where the wind can pass through.

Here, the command is not a summary. It's a **philosophical tension, compressed into action.**

Writing Strong Commands

Encourage students to:

- Use **verbs** that imply transformation or choice.
- Avoid "you should" or "always."

- Let the command deepen the paradox—not flatten it.

Don't explain.
Don't moralize.
Don't answer.
Push.

Using Pressure System in the Classroom

This book was designed with versatility in mind. Whether you're teaching a full creative writing course or integrating poetry into a broader curriculum, Pressure System supports a wide range of instructional goals.

Structure of the Book

Each entry includes:

- A **poem**, built on a looped or recursive logic
- A **paradox** triad (implied or embedded)
- A final **command** line, distilling the emotional or philosophical charge

Suggested Classroom Approaches

1. Reading as Inquiry
Use the poems as short, dense prompts for close reading.

- What's happening here?
- What's missing?
- What shifted?

Encourage students to **generate multiple** interpretations before settling into analysis.

2. Writing in Response

Assign triad-based poems of students' own:

- Begin with a paradox (e.g., vanish / return / altered)
- Anchor it in a physical system
- Compress into a short, structured loop

3. Triad Mapping

Have students extract or invent paradox triads from existing poems or essays. This reinforces both analytical and creative skills.

4. Command Creation

After reading a poem, students write their own command line—then compare with the book's. What changed? Why?

Flexibility

Pressure System can be:

- A **primary text** in a poetry-focused course

- A **creative anchor** in interdisciplinary units (e.g., science + literature)

- A **supplementary tool** in writing, rhetoric, or even philosoph

The Pressure System: A Brief Theoretical Framework

Pressure System is built on a foundational question:

What happens when we compress experience until only structure remains?

This approach is neither confessional nor abstract. It privileges form, tension, and recursion over metaphor or narrative. The result is a poetry of paradox — one that invites precision without demanding closure.

Core Principles

1. Paradox Triads

Each poem emerges from a triad: three nodes in conflict or sequence, often unresolved.

Example:
Start / Middle / Gone — a triad exploring time as motion and vanishing.

Triads can be spatial, emotional, scientific, or entirely linguistic. What matters is tension among the three — not symmetry, not resolution.

2. Compression

These poems are small, but not minimal. Each one compresses an entire system into a few lines. The compression is purposeful: to increase pressure — and in turn, clarity.

3. Looping Logic

Rather than linear progression, many poems employ recursion or echo. The beginning returns, altered. Or the structure loops forward, backward, or inward. This reflects how memory, trauma, wonder — and science — often work.

4. Anti-Metaphor

These poems do not symbolize experience; they reveal its mechanics. A glacier is not like repression — it is repression, in form. The reader is asked to observe, not translate.

Outcomes

Students reading and writing under this system learn to:

- Notice structure and contradiction in natural and human systems

- Write with precision, restraint, and consequence

- Embrace ambiguity without collapsing into vagueness

- Develop resilience through design

How to Read a Pressure System Poem

These poems resist easy interpretation. They are not puzzles to solve, nor confessions to decode. Instead, they are compressed systems — built from pressure, pattern, and paradox. To read them well, slow down. Read them more than once.

Step 1: Observe, Don't Translate

Avoid the impulse to "figure out what it means." Begin instead by asking:

- What is literally happening?
- What natural or physical process is being described?
- Where does tension appear — in structure, sound, or idea?

Step 2: Locate the Triad

Each poem is built around a paradox triad — a system of three interrelated nodes. Sometimes the triad is obvious; sometimes it is buried in motion, material, or implication.

Ask:

- What are the three key moments, objects, or forces?
- How are they related: by transformation, conflict, decay, recursion?

- Does something vanish, return, or reappear altered?

Step 3: Note Compression and Loop

Look for structural pressure. Compression might appear in:

- Line length
- Image density
- Elided connections
- Abrupt shifts

Looping may be subtle — a return of language, tone, or concept. A reappearance that is not repetition.

Step 4: Engage the Command

Each poem ends with a "command." These are not moral instructions. They are provocations — invitations to respond, extend, or embody the system.

Ask:

- Who is the command speaking to?
- What kind of action or awareness does it call for?
- Is it in alignment with the poem, or in tension?

Step 5: Respond Through Design

Rather than summarize or explain the poem, try to build something from it:

- A variation using the same triad
- A physical system that mirrors the pressure
- A diagram, sound loop, or gesture that embodies the tension

Reading is not extraction. It is continuation.

Using Pressure System in the Classroom

This book is not a unit. It is a tool. It's not meant to be taught in a single week, or even a single semester. Instead, it offers a pressure-based approach to poetic and conceptual thinking that can thread through multiple courses: composition, literature, philosophy, design, ecology, or creative writing.

Below are ways to integrate the text into classroom use — for students at the college level and beyond.

1. Begin with Observation, Not Interpretation

Ask students to read a single poem aloud. No questions, no commentary. Then again. Then again.

Prompts:

- What three things are physically happening?
- Where is the pressure? The fracture?
- If this poem were a system diagram, what would the nodes be?

Let students linger in description before assigning "meaning."

2. Use the Triads Across Disciplines

Each poem's paradox triad allows for interdisciplinary inquiry.

In **science**: Model the triad using a real-world physical, ecological, or anatomical system.

In **design or engineering**: Trace how pressure moves through form.

In **philosophy or ethics**: Analyze how conflicting forces create moral, perceptual, or existential tension.

In art or music: Translate a triad into visual composition or sonic variation.

3. Teach the Command Line as Compression

Each command is a distilled reaction — not to the content of the poem, but to the system it implies.

Ask students to write their own command line:

- Based on their reading of a poem
- In response to their own lived experience
- As a revision to an existing poem's command

Let them treat the command as the pressure valve — the place where meaning becomes motion.

4. Assign Poetic Variations

Students can be asked to:

- Write a poem using the same triad with different materials

- Construct a loop poem where only the verb shifts
- Compress an entire system (political, biological, emotional) into 8–10 lines, without metaphor or explanation

Encourage precision. Eliminate glue words. Remove "I." Push toward structural integrity.

5. Encourage Cross-Pollination

Because the poems are rooted in natural phenomena, they invite research. Let students:

- Investigate a concept (e.g., tectonic shift, neuroplasticity, fungal networks)
- Identify a paradox or triad within that system
- Translate that into a new poem or microtext

They don't need to be scientists — but they do need to observe like one.

Pressure Systems and Writing Across the Curriculum

Though Pressure System is rooted in poetic form, its structure lends itself to broader writing instruction. By framing emotional, ecological, and conceptual states as systems under pressure, this book supports multiple pedagogical goals:

1. Teaching Compression and Precision

In disciplines where word count is limited — grant writing, journalism, executive summaries, abstracts — Pressure System trains students to:

- Cut excess language
- Replace generalities with specificity
- Understand how structure generates clarity

Use any poem in the book as a model for compact, layered expression. Ask students: What happens when we remove this word? Change the order? Does the system still hold?

2. Strengthening Systems Thinking

Many fields — from ecology to economics — depend on understanding how forces move through systems.

Each poem in this book illustrates:

- Input → Pressure → Change
- Cause → Reaction → Residue

- Force → Fracture → Form

Students can map these flows in both textual and visual form, building an interdisciplinary habit of system-awareness.

3. Encouraging Ambiguity with Accountability

Unlike argument-driven writing, many forms of inquiry require students to:

- Pose layered questions
- Acknowledge uncertainty
- Explore multiple interpretations without collapsing them into thesis

Pressure System models a kind of responsible ambiguity: poems that leave space, yet offer precision. The triads help students articulate what's happening — even if "why" remains open.

4. Connecting Observation to Insight

Academic writing often collapses too quickly into "point-making." These poems slow that instinct down.

Encourage students to:

- Watch first. Think second. Interpret last.
- Move from object to system to self.
- Write from the edge of certainty, not its center.

Pressure System is not about "expressing yourself" — it's about understanding what self-expression must press against.

On Loop Structure and the Poetics of Return

Each poem in Pressure System follows a looped structure: a form that returns to itself with difference. Rather than relying on linear progression, these loops emphasize recurrence, distortion, and variation — principles found across both natural systems and emotional states.

1. Why Loops?

Loops offer a structural model for:

- **Repetition** with change — echoing how emotion, memory, and even trauma work

- **Cyclical logic** — mirroring seasons, biological processes, and weather patterns

- **Compression and resonance** — creating meaning through rhythm, recursion, and contrast

In contrast to climactic narrative arcs, loops resist finality. They end by returning.

2. Loop = Form of Thinking

Students often assume poems must "build" to something or "mean" something directly. The loop resists that. It teaches students to:

- Value nuance over conclusion
- Find tension in what doesn't resolve

- Listen for return, resonance, and rhythm

Ask: What changes in the repetition? What doesn't? What does that shift do?

3. Loops and Reader Responsibility

Because each looped poem is stripped of overt metaphor, the reader must do more interpretive work. The return structures ask:

- What is being mirrored?
- What's lost in the return?
- What emotional or systemic pressure caused the change?

These are questions of critical reading — essential across disciplines.

4. How to Teach the Loop

Try these approaches:

- **Annotate the triad**: Ask students to identify the start, turn, and return in the poem.

- **Visual mapping:** Have students draw the "shape" of the poem's motion — where does it loop? Fracture? Recoil?

- **Model across texts**: Compare loop structures to biological cycles, mechanical feedback loops, historical patterns, etc.

The loop is a form that connects across fields —
poetic, cognitive, scientific, and personal.

How to Teach Compression without Symbolism

Many students are trained to read poetry symbolically: the rose = love, the crow = death, and so on. In Pressure System, we ask them to do something harder — and, perhaps, more meaningful: to read without the crutch of fixed metaphor.

1. What Is Compression?

Compression is the reduction of language without the reduction of force. In a compressed poem:

- Every word bears weight.
- Meaning arises from juxtaposition, not explanation.
- Interpretation is activated, not delivered.

This teaches students precision as a form of empathy — the ability to say more with less, and trust the reader to meet them there.

2. Why Not Symbolism?

Symbolism asks: What does this represent?

Compression asks: What does this do?

By removing explicit metaphor, these poems:

- Avoid cliché
- Honor the material world in its own strangeness

- Encourage observation over projection

Students learn to trust image, sound, and structure — not just "meaning."

3. Techniques for Teaching Compression

Try the following:

- **Word-for-word breakdowns**: Ask students why each word is there. Could anything be removed? Why not?

- **One-sentence summaries**: After reading a poem, challenge students to describe it in a single, compressed sentence.

- **Reverse engineering:** Pick a poem and expand it — then compress it again. What's lost? What's gained?

4. What Students Learn

Teaching compression trains:

- Precision
- Critical thinking
- Aesthetic sensitivity
- Emotional resilience (through indirect expression)

It's not about solving a poem — it's about sitting with it. Watching what shifts under pressure.

On Triads and Systematic Emotion

Pressure System uses a framework of triads—three-word constellations—to create a compositional and interpretive structure that moves beyond metaphor. These triads are not merely themes; they are pressure points where perception, language, and emotional resonance converge.

1. What Is a Triad?

Each triad consists of three components:

- A **starting force** (e.g., spark, fracture, arrival)

- A **complicating presence** (e.g., echo, gravity, hesitation)

- A **resulting form** (e.g., shadow, absence, eruption)

These are not metaphors — they are phenomena. Each triad invites a pattern of tension, transformation, and release.

2. Triads as Emotional Architecture

Instead of saying, "This poem is about grief," we ask:

- What physical system mirrors grief?
- What natural event reflects its behavior?
- What pressure causes it to move, change, or break?

Triads give students a way to **construct** emotion rather than simply name it.

3. Using Triads in Class

You can invite students to:

- **Identify the triad**: What are the three pressures or forces in the poem?

- **Remix the triad**: Swap out one term and see how the emotional trajectory shifts.

- **Write from a triad:** Begin with three physical phenomena (e.g., ice, crack, flood) and write a poem that moves through them.

4. Triads and Critical Thinking

Because triads are not symbols, students must:

- Observe more closely
- Draw unexpected connections
- Accept ambiguity without surrendering inquiry

This fosters **resilience in meaning-making** — a skill crucial to reading, writing, and life beyond the classroom.

How to Read a Poem Without Solving It

Many students approach poetry like a puzzle with a single correct answer. But Pressure System invites a different stance: not to solve the poem, but to stay with it.

1. There Is No Code to Crack

This book avoids metaphor in the traditional sense. A "knife" isn't secretly love. A "seed" isn't secretly loss. These images are exactly what they are—but placed under pressure.

Ask students:

- What's happening physically?
- What forces are interacting?
- What system is being revealed?

Meaning lives in the structure, not in hidden symbolism.

2. Poems as Systems, Not Symbols

Each poem is an emotional system expressed through a physical process. If students can:

- describe the system,
- trace its tension and release,
- and witness its transformation,

then they've understood the poem—whether or not they've "decoded" it.

3. Don't Fix the Poem—Feel It Move

Encourage students to:

- Sit with ambiguity
- Resist closure
- Let meaning accumulate, not appear all at once

and Some poems will click immediately. Others will unfold over days. This is a feature, not a flaw.

4. Use the Paratexts

Each poem includes:

- A triad
- A scientific or natural context
- Discussion prompts
- Creative response ideas

These are not answers—they're ways in.

On Emotion, Precision, and Pressure

In this book, emotion is not expressed through personal confession or ornate metaphor. Instead, it emerges through precision under pressure—through systems.

Emotion as Compression

We don't always express emotion in words. Sometimes we express it by:

- standing still when we want to run,
- laughing too loud in a silent room,
- watching a tree shed its bark.

These moments contain feeling—not in what they say, but in what they hold.

That's compression.

Pressure Systems

Every poem in this collection is built around a **pressure system**:

- Tension builds
- Something breaks or transforms
- A new state emerges

The physical world provides endless models for this emotional dynamic. Geysers, gravity wells, tectonic faults—each mirrors our inner processes.

We don't liken a breakup to a landslide. We show a landslide and let the reader feel the break.

Precision is = Care

Precision is not cold.

To name things carefully—whether it's a tree species, a weather event, or a behavior in animals—is an act of **attention**, and therefore **love**.

This book asks students to be precise in their seeing, careful in their naming, and brave in their willingness to sit inside paradox.

What Is a Loop Poem?

A **loop poem** uses structure—not metaphor—to reveal emotional complexity.

Each loop poem in this book is based on a paradox triad: a system of three forces or moments that seem contradictory but coexist.

The Structure

A loop poem moves in three phases:

1. **Tension builds**
2. **A break or shift occurs**
3. **A residue remains**

This movement reflects physical, psychological, and emotional pressure systems. But unlike traditional poetry forms, the loop poem is not bound by rhyme, meter, or even narrative.

It is bound by **pressure**.

The Triad

Each poem begins with a triad, a sequence of three terms that guide the movement. For example:

- **Contain / Press / Bloom**
- **Stillness / Impact / Dispersal**
- **Gather / Twist / Release**

These aren't metaphors. They're descriptive forces. Think of them like variables in a natural system.

Example:

Let's say your triad is:

Stillness / Impact / Dispersal

Your poem might begin with a quiet scene, introduce a sudden action (like a drop or strike), and end with particles, ripples, or something scattering. You don't explain it. You show it.

The result?

A poem that feels like anxiety, or awe, or love—without ever using those words.

No Metaphor, No Problem

We avoid simile and metaphor not because they are "bad," but because they often explain too much. Loop poems invite the reader to encounter the feeling—not be told what to feel.

Instructor Preface

This edition exists to reduce preparation, not to prescribe instruction.

The student edition of Pressure System contains only the poems, presented without commentary. Students encounter the work directly, without prompts or interpretive framing. This Instructor Edition includes the same poems, supplemented with optional structural notes and discussion prompts.

These materials are not explanations. They are tools for redirecting attention when discussion stalls or defaults to familiar habits.

The prompts focus on structure, process, and pressure rather than theme or symbolism. They are designed to support the teaching of non-narrative poetry without requiring specialized theory or extensive advance planning. A poem may be taught with no reference to the accompanying material, or with selective use of a single prompt.

Nothing in this edition is meant to be covered in full.

Use what is useful. Ignore the rest.
The poems do not depend on this material to function.

This book does not ask for correct interpretation. It asks for careful observation. The instructional material exists only to help sustain that attention.

The goal is not resolution, but contact.

Foreword

What would it mean to teach poems that do not ask to be decoded?
The poems in Pressure System are not organized around theme, speaker, or metaphor. They operate as compressed fields of action: physical, cognitive, ecological, mechanical. Meaning does not unfold through explanation or narrative progression, but through contact—through attention held under strain.

This presents a familiar classroom problem. When poems refuse symbolism and resist paraphrase, discussion often collapses into either personal association or interpretive guessing. Both responses are understandable. Neither is required here.

The work in this book asks for a different mode of engagement: observation before interpretation, structure before statement. Images do not stand in for something else; they behave. Language functions less as representation than as pressure—accumulating, deferring, transferring.

This is not a rejection of interpretation, but a delay of it. Students are asked first to notice what happens: how forces accumulate, how systems stall, where release occurs, where it doesn't. The poems reward that patience.

The instructional materials that follow do not explain the poems. They offer points of entry when needed—ways to sustain attention, redirect discussion, or name structural features without closing them down. They are optional by design.

Used lightly, this book supports the teaching of contemporary poetry, ecopoetics, lyric compression, and non-narrative form. Used minimally, it asks only that students read closely and stay with difficulty longer than usual.

The poems will do the rest.
2026

Author's Note

These poems are built from real processes: physical, ecological, mechanical, anatomical. Nothing here is invented. Many of the terms may sound unfamiliar or poetic, but they are literal. If something feels strange, it is often because the process itself is unfamiliar, not because it is symbolic.

Each poem forms around a pressure point—a condition where forces meet without resolving. Some pressures stabilize briefly. Others rupture or transfer. The poems do not explain these outcomes. They stop where the system holds or fails.

The work avoids narrative, speaker, and metaphor by design. Images do not stand in for ideas. They operate. Language functions less as description than as compression.

The book is arranged in three phases—Conditions, Tensions, and Echoes—not as themes, but as states of force. Matter accumulates. Mind intervenes. Being emerges, destabilizes, and presses back against the system.

Nothing here is meant to be decoded. Reading is not a puzzle to solve, but an act of sustained

attention. The poems reward patience more than interpretation.
They are not asking what something means. They are asking what happens when pressure is applied.

*"The structure holds.
Whether you do is not a concern."*

I. Conditions

Structural Use (Optional) — Hayflick

Possible Entry

One possible way into the poem is to remain with the opening images as literal processes and resist treating them symbolically.

Discussion Prompts (as useful)

- What kinds of processes are juxtaposed here, and where do they appear to operate on different scales?
- Where does the poem shift from observation toward compression rather than development?
- How does the poem handle beginnings and endings—what starts, what breaks, and what never stabilizes?
- Which elements feel as though they are placed under strain rather than explained?
- How does the poem's pressure change if any single image is removed?

Pressure

- The poem may be approached by attending to how pressure is generated through accumulation rather than progression.
- The ending can be treated as a structural stop rather than a resolution.

Optional Compositional Extension

- A related exercise might involve placing several literal processes side by side without clarifying their relationship.
- Allow the poem to end at the point where further connection would force explanation.
- The poem may stop where pressure remains intact.

Hayflick

Redwood on reef
spit out—
white smoker.

A battery powered sponge
exhales,
hot air—
cool ocean gurgles.

A germ
teetering dawn,
oogonia dusk,
a clock explodes—

cracked eggs.

Structural Use (Optional) — Umfeld

Possible Entry

One way into the poem is to remain with the physical action at the opening and delay interpretation.

Discussion Prompts (as useful)

- What tensions are set in motion by the opening image, and which of them remain unresolved?
- Where does the language shift away from physical action toward cognitive or reflexive phrasing?
- At what point does thought appear to loop or stall? What words mark that change?
- How does the act of measurement near the end function here? What does it fail to stabilize?
- How does the pressure change if the final lines are removed? How does it change if the opening image is removed?

Pressure

- The poem can be approached by tracking whether pressure accumulates through compression or pivots through shifts in register.
- The ending may be treated as a stopping point rather than a conclusion.

Optional Compositional Extension

- A related exercise might begin with a literal physical action.
- Allow a brief moment where cognition enters.
- End with an attempted act of measurement that cannot resolve what precedes it.
- The poem may stop where pressure holds.

Umfeld

A frozen tongue,
toe,

polishing—
faint trickling,

brine—
rusty river.

A mind
stuck between poles,
floating over a hole.

Smoothed over a coastline,
a circle of footprints—

I measure eternity
with a sock.

Structural Use (Optional) — Cracked Shells

Possible Entry
One way into the poem is to attend to the repeated phrase and consider how it functions structurally rather than thematically.

Discussion Prompts (as useful)

- What kinds of cycles or recurrences are suggested by the repeated phrase, and where do they differ rather than align?
- How do the poem's images relate through placement rather than sequence?
- Where does motion appear, and how is it interrupted or redirected?
- What forms of support or transfer are present, and where do they operate without explanation?
- How does the pressure change if the repeated phrase is removed or altered?

Pressure

- The poem can be approached by observing how pressure is generated through return rather than progression.
- The ending may be treated as a re-entry point rather than a conclusion.

Optional Compositional Extension

- A related exercise might involve placing a recurring phrase within a poem so that its function shifts with each appearance.
- Allow images to connect through adjacency rather than narrative logic.
- The poem may stop where recurrence holds without resolution.

Cracked Shells

Cracked shells—
rock bed in a dry creek—
crow caw.

Mother tree feeds
a sapling sprout—
nurse log.

Moonlit boil lumbering
downslope—
grip,
flip—

cracked shells.

Structural Use (Optional) — Ballast

Possible Entry
One way into the poem is to notice how images associated with support or balance appear in compromised or unstable forms.

Discussion Prompts (as useful)

- What kinds of support or grounding are suggested by the images, and where do they appear insufficient?
- How do the images relate through function rather than sequence or narrative?
- Where does the poem remain external and physical, and where does a more reflexive register briefly enter?
- What forms of failure are present without being resolved or explained?
- How does the pressure change if the final image is removed? How does it change if the opening image is removed?

Pressure

- The poem can be approached by attending to how pressure is sustained through precarious equilibrium rather than motion or development.
- The ending may be treated as a point where stability gives way without transition.

Optional Compositional Extension

- A related exercise might involve assembling images that imply balance, support, or ballast, allowing each to fail differently.
- Connections may remain functional rather than interpretive.
- The poem may stop where instability holds.

Ballast

A flanked ass,
heaps of hay—
three-legged stand.

A ladder
jutting a ditch,
slumped in mud—
I chat with a shadow.

A broken keel—
waft of wind—

turtled.

Structural Use (Optional) — Still Dangling

Possible Entry
One way into the poem is to attend to states of suspension and near-motion, noting where action is implied but deferred.

Discussion Prompts (as useful)

- What forms of attachment or dependence appear here, and where do they remain unresolved?
- How does the poem handle stillness alongside pressure or force?
- Where does interruption occur, and how does it differ from breakage or completion?
- How do repetition and variation function across the poem's images?
- How does the pressure change if the repeated element is removed or altered?

Pressure

- The poem may be approached by observing how pressure is sustained through delay rather than progression.
- The ending can be treated as a shift in condition rather than a release.

Optional Compositional Extension

- A related exercise might involve placing an image of suspension beside an image of strain or fracture.
- Allow repetition to introduce variation without resolution.
- The poem may stop where suspension persists or begins to destabilize.

Still Dangling

Porcupine gaze—
pawpaw dangling—
still.

Nip-twig—
cracked bone.

Wind—
pawpaw dangling—

wobbling.

Structural Use (Optional) — Kettle Lake

Possible Entry
One way into the poem is to attend to how slow, cumulative processes are named without being narrativized.

Discussion Prompts (as useful)

- What kinds of forces are present here, and how do they differ in scale or duration?
- How does the poem handle movement that is incremental rather than directional?
- Where does the language remain purely process-based, and where does naming intervene?
- How do gaps, pauses, or breaks in the lines contribute to pressure?
- How does the pressure change if the final naming is removed? How does it change if the opening processes are removed?

Pressure

- The poem may be approached by observing how pressure accumulates through duration rather than event.
- The ending can be treated as a settling rather than a resolution.

Optional Compositional Extension

- A related exercise might involve listing forces acting on a landscape or object over time.
- Allow process to remain visible without explanation or metaphor.
- The poem may stop at the point where accumulation holds.

Kettle Lake

Swollen frozen cracks,
shards of slate,
a glacier plucks a rockhead.

Plodding, slogging,
scraping,
deep gaping—

rain, sun,
an ocean breeze—
kettle lake.

Structural Use (Optional) — Snow Sheath

Possible Entry

One way into the poem is to attend to layers of covering and containment, noting how each layer both protects and constrains.

Discussion Prompts (as useful)

- What kinds of coverings or enclosures appear, and what do they obscure or preserve?
- How does the poem move through layers rather than forward in time?
- Where does an external action intervene, and how does it alter what was sealed?
- How do hardness and fragility coexist across the images?
- How does the pressure change if the final image is removed? How does it change if the intervening action is removed?

Pressure

- The poem may be approached by observing how pressure is generated through compression and containment.
- The ending can be treated as exposure rather than resolution.

Optional Compositional Extension

- A related exercise might involve constructing a poem through successive layers, each enclosing the next.
- Allow an action to breach the surface without explanation.
- The poem may stop where containment gives way.

Snow Sheath

Packed snow
over ice—

shoveler sheathes
a blade—

bone-jar.

Structural Use (Optional) — Playa Bloom

Possible Entry

One way into the poem is to attend to how conditions of excess and absence are placed side by side without mediation.

Discussion Prompts (as useful)

- What opposing environments are suggested, and how are they held together without transition?
- How does the poem handle emergence in a context that resists it?
- Where does the language register saturation, and where does it register depletion?
- How does the final image reframe or withdraw from what precedes it?
- What happens to the poem's pressure if either environment is removed?

Pressure

- The poem may be approached by observing how pressure is generated through contrast rather than accumulation.
- The ending can be treated as a displacement rather than a conclusion.

Optional Compositional Extension

- A related exercise might involve placing an image of abundance beside an image of scarcity.
- Allow the relationship between them to remain unarticulated.
- The poem may stop where contrast holds without synthesis.

Playa Bloom

Inflated flowers,
wet rock—
bloom.

Arid air,
cracked playa—

tumbleweed.

Structural Use (Optional) — June Gloom

Possible Entry
One way into the poem is to attend to how distance is measured and remeasured without arriving at a fixed point.

Discussion Prompts (as useful)

- How does the poem handle movement toward a horizon that remains unreachable?
- What effect does numerical division have on the sense of progression or proximity?
- Where do solidity and insubstantiality coexist across the images?
- How do repetition and reduction function differently in the first and second halves of the poem?
- What changes if the poem is read as circling rather than advancing?

Pressure

- The poem may be approached by observing how pressure is sustained through continual deferral.
- The ending can be treated as a return to condition rather than a conclusion.

Optional Compositional Extension

- A related exercise might involve approaching a distant object through successive reductions.
- Allow movement to be implied without arrival.
- The poem may stop where distance persists.

June Gloom

Swelling hull,
waves unfold
waves,
blue heeled horizon—

half the way,
a quarter,
an eighth…

Phantom islands,
whispering winds.

Structural Use (Optional) — Zero Shadow Day

Possible Entry
One way into the poem is to attend to conditions where contrast briefly collapses or becomes indistinguishable.

Discussion Prompts (as useful)

- What elements here depend on light, reflection, or alignment rather than movement?
- How does the poem handle visibility when shadow is absent or minimized?
- Where do natural and manufactured materials come into contact?
- How does the central condition affect scale or orientation?
- What changes if the moment of alignment is treated as fleeting rather than stable?

Pressure

- The poem may be approached by observing how pressure is generated through precision and alignment rather than accumulation.
- The ending can be treated as a residual effect rather than an outcome.

Optional Compositional Extension

- A related exercise might involve describing a moment when contrast briefly disappears.
- Allow attention to rest on surfaces, reflections, or glints without explanation.
- The poem may stop where alignment disperses.

Zero Shadow Day

A glass fir,
shimmering nest
egg—

zero shadow day—
preen oil on cullet—

glints.

Structural Use (Optional) — Iteration

Possible Entry
One way into the poem is to attend to how repetition functions as movement rather than emphasis.

Discussion Prompts (as useful)

- How does the poem generate forward motion through recurrence rather than progression?
- What changes as phrases repeat, and what remains fixed?
- How do rhythm and sound carry pressure independently of imagery?
- Where does effort register physically, and how is direction established or resisted?
- How does the introduction of invented or abstract destination affect the sense of climb?

Pressure

- The poem may be approached by observing how pressure is sustained through iterative motion rather than accumulation.
- The ending can be treated as an intensification of pattern rather than a conclusion.

Optional Compositional Extension

- A related exercise might involve writing a poem built from a repeated phrase that gradually shifts context or register.
- Allow rhythm to carry movement even as language loops.
- The poem may stop where iteration exhausts itself rather than resolves.

Iteration

Et cetera, et cetera,
up the schefflera I go!
The leaf is thin, the stem is green,
the space is narrow in between,
but up and up I go.

And so on, and so forth,
and henceforth, and thenceforth—
the gravity is pulling south,
the climb is tasting in my mouth,
as to the north I go.

Et cetera, et cetera,
the vine is stretching like a wire—
so on and so forth,
and henceforth and thenceforth,
into the Quarth I go…

Et cetera!

Structural Use (Optional) — Ironwood

Possible Entry
One way into the poem is to attend to how density is established through compression rather than description.

Discussion Prompts (as useful)

- What kinds of material qualities are foregrounded, and how are they conveyed with minimal language?
- How do sound and texture function in place of narrative or movement?
- Where does shadow operate as substance rather than absence?
- How does the poem's brevity affect the pressure it generates?
- What shifts if any single element is removed?

Pressure

- The poem may be approached by observing how pressure is concentrated through reduction.
- The ending can be treated as a terminal density rather than an opening.

Optional Compositional Extension

- A related exercise might involve compressing a poem to its most materially resonant elements.
- Allow sound, texture, or density to carry meaning without elaboration.
- The poem may stop where further reduction would dissipate pressure.

Ironwood

Ironwood—
gritty wind—
resin shadows.

Structural Use (Optional) — Step Leader

Possible Entry
One way into the poem is to attend to how conditions are established before action occurs, and how action arrives only after prolonged suspension.

Discussion Prompts (as useful)

- What states or conditions are named prior to any discharge or event?
- How does the poem distinguish between gradual buildup and sudden release?
- Where does movement remain directional without completion?
- How do technical terms function alongside elemental imagery?
- How does the pressure change if the final sound is removed? How does it change if the buildup is shortened?

Pressure

- The poem may be approached by observing how pressure accumulates invisibly before manifesting abruptly.
- The ending can be treated as an event rather than a resolution.

Optional Compositional Extension

- A related exercise might involve establishing atmospheric or conditional states before allowing a single decisive action.
- Allow technical or process language to coexist with sensory description.
- The poem may stop at the moment of discharge.

Boom

Air—
clear,
cloudy—
quiescent.

Updrafts and downdrafts,
ground shadows—

step leader—
upward streamer—
return stroke—

Structural Use (Optional) — Bread

Possible Entry

One way into the poem is to attend to how sequential processes are presented without narrative framing or explanation.

Discussion Prompts (as useful)

- What stages or transformations are implied, and how are they marked linguistically?
- How does the poem handle time—where is it measured, and where is it only suggested?
- What roles do heat and pressure play across the poem's movement?
- Where do sound cues intervene, and how do they function structurally?
- How does the final naming alter or consolidate what precedes it?

Pressure

- The poem may be approached by observing how pressure accumulates through preparation rather than action.
- The ending can be treated as a convergence rather than a conclusion.

Optional Compositional Extension

- A related exercise might involve listing the stages of a familiar process without narrating them.
- Allow sound or timing cues to signal change instead of explanation.
- The poem may stop where transformation is implied but not depicted.

Bread

Flour well—
cracked eggs,

A cold kettle hisses—
roiling,
boiling,

whistling—
a clock beeps…

Structural Use (Optional) — Lee Side

Possible Entry
One way into the poem is to attend to how force behaves when partially blocked or redirected rather than stopped.

Discussion Prompts (as useful)

- What forms of shelter or resistance are suggested, and where do they prove incomplete?
- How does the poem handle movement that is turbulent rather than linear?
- Where does force "bleed through" instead of breaking cleanly?
- How do scale shifts operate between landscape and branch?
- How does the pressure change as motion narrows toward a single point?

Pressure

- The poem may be approached by observing how pressure concentrates through deflection rather than direct impact.
- The ending can be treated as a localized release rather than a full discharge.

Optional Compositional Extension

- A related exercise might involve describing the effects of force acting indirectly on an object.
- Allow movement to register through bending, eddying, or bleed-through rather than collision.
- The poem may stop where redirection gives way to snap.

Lee Side

Lee side tumbling,
eddies break a bluff—
bleeding crown.

Folded branch,
flat leaves—
a narrow cone
bends with a gust—

snap.

II. Tensions

Structural Use (Optional) — Lydian

Possible Entry
One way into the poem is to attend to how small physical actions generate patterned outcomes.

Discussion Prompts (as useful)

- What role does breath or airflow play before any intentional action occurs?
- How does the poem move from physical mechanism to ordered sequence?
- Where does repetition become structure rather than emphasis?
- How do technical terms interact with sensory description?
- What changes if the final naming is removed? What changes if it is foregrounded earlier?

Pressure

- The poem may be approached by observing how pressure is shaped through controlled release rather than force.
- The ending can be treated as a designation rather than a resolution.

Optional Compositional Extension

- A related exercise might involve tracing a physical action as it produces an ordered pattern.
- Allow terminology to appear late, after the process is already underway.
- The poem may stop where structure becomes audible or legible.

Lydian

A pulse of air,
ricocheting—
conical bore.

I press a key—
two,
now three.

A broken reed—
a major scale—

raised fourth.

Structural Use (Optional) — Dotted Line

Possible Entry
One way into the poem is to attend to how repetition frames containment rather than development.

Discussion Prompts (as useful)

- What forms of enclosure or control are suggested by the repeated self-descriptions?
- How does the poem handle identity through objects or systems rather than narrative?
- Where does the act of marking or signing appear, and what does it defer or suspend?
- How does repetition function as boundary rather than emphasis?
- What changes if the middle image is removed? What changes if the repetition is altered?

Pressure

- The poem may be approached by observing how pressure is generated through self-containment rather than motion.
- The ending can be treated as a return to constraint rather than closure.

Optional Compositional Extension

- A related exercise might involve repeating a self-description with a single intervening action or object.
- Allow the act of inscription to remain incomplete.
- The poem may stop where the boundary is reaffirmed rather than crossed.

Dotted Line

I am a glass cage—
Windsor knot,
side-part.

Fresh pen,
my trembling hand—
a blank dotted line.

Black box—
Windsor knot,
side-part.

Structural Use (Optional) — Laid Out

Possible Entry

One way into the poem is to attend to how placement and arrangement function in place of action.

Discussion Prompts (as useful)

- What kinds of ordering or preparation are suggested by the listed objects?
- How does the poem handle presence through what is laid out rather than who appears?
- Where does stillness dominate, and how is it briefly disturbed?
- How do sound and settling operate as markers of time?
- What changes if the final stanza is removed? What changes if the inventory is shortened?

Pressure

- The poem may be approached by observing how pressure is generated through suspension and quiet accumulation.
- The ending can be treated as a settling rather than a release.

Optional Compositional Extension

- A related exercise might involve arranging personal or impersonal objects without explaining their significance.
- Allow a single, minor disturbance to register against stillness.
- The poem may stop where motion subsides and arrangement holds.

Laid Out

A coat,
hat,
a cashmere sweater—
draped over a cameo.
Wrinkled tie,
point collar—
folded galluses
tucked in a shoe.

I sit—
a floorboard squeaks—

dust
settles.

Structural Use (Optional) — Long Roll

Possible Entry

One way into the poem is to attend to how repetition functions through variation rather than return.

Discussion Prompts (as useful)

- What changes as the repeated action recurs, and what remains constant?
- How does the poem register motion through sound and touch rather than image?
- Where does control give way to vibration or flutter?
- How does the body enter the poem indirectly, through sensation rather than description?
- What shifts if the final return is removed? What shifts if the opening phrase is withheld?

Pressure

- The poem may be approached by observing how pressure is sustained through continuous modulation rather than escalation.
- The ending can be treated as a continuation rather than a closure.

Optional Compositional Extension

- A related exercise might involve sustaining a repeated action while allowing small physical variations to accumulate.
- Let rhythm carry structure without narrative support.
- The poem may stop where repetition persists rather than resolves.

Long Roll

Taps—
level,
bouncing on a drum.

Swollen sheaths,
a tingling thumb—

taps—
rugged—
fluttering on drum.

Structural Use (Optional) — Holdfasts

Possible Entry
One way into the poem is to attend to how anchoring and movement are held in proximity without hierarchy.

Discussion Prompts (as useful)

- What forms of attachment or grounding are suggested, and how are they described materially?
- How does the poem balance upward pull and lateral motion?
- Where does flexibility function as stability rather than weakness?
- How do the terms for structure contrast with the terms for motion?
- What changes if either the anchoring elements or the drifting elements are removed?

Pressure

- The poem may be approached by observing how pressure is maintained through simultaneous holding and yielding.
- The ending can be treated as continued motion rather than release or resolution.

Optional Compositional Extension

- A related exercise might involve placing an image of anchoring beside an image of drift.
- Allow both forces to remain active without reconciliation.
- The poem may stop where tension between holding and movement persists.

Holdfasts

Holdfasts—
rounded pillows—
surge.

Gas bladders undulate,
upright rubber stipe—

drift.

Structural Use (Optional) — Crystallography

Possible Entry
One way into the poem is to attend to how pattern arises through repetition and symmetry rather than intention.

Discussion Prompts (as useful)

- What kinds of structures or lattices are suggested, and how are they assembled incrementally?
- How does mirroring or reflection function across the poem's phrases?
- Where do dryness and moisture operate as competing conditions?
- How do shifts in scale move from abstraction toward aggregation?
- What changes if the final consolidation is removed? What changes if it appears earlier?

Pressure

- The poem may be approached by observing how pressure accumulates through alignment and repetition.
- The ending can be treated as a convergence rather than a resolution.

Optional Compositional Extension

- A related exercise might involve repeating a simple form while allowing environmental conditions to alter it.
- Allow pattern to emerge without explanation.
- The poem may stop where accumulation becomes visible.

Crystallography

Six-sided
desert dust—
cold lattice,
prism.

Arm reflects
arm, reflects
air—

dry pockets,
wet drafts—

thin needles,
flat plate—

a clump of ice.

Structural Use (Optional) — Camera Click

Possible Entry

One way into the poem is to attend to how observation itself alters what is observed.

Discussion Prompts (as useful)

- What conditions are implied before and after the act of measurement?
- How does the poem position observation as an intervention rather than a record?
- Where does reduction replace accumulation?
- How do the paired images function without causal explanation?
- What changes if the act of recording is treated as erasure rather than capture?

Pressure

- The poem may be approached by observing how pressure emerges through collapse rather than buildup.
- The ending can be treated as a remainder rather than a conclusion.

Optional Compositional Extension

- A related exercise might involve placing an act of observation beside its unintended consequence.
- Allow the moment of measurement to alter the field it measures.
- The poem may stop where certainty dissolves.

Camera Click

A double slit—
camera click.

A memory erased—
waves.

Structural Use (Optional) — Callus

Possible Entry
One way into the poem is to attend to how repetition produces structural change over time rather than immediate effect.

Discussion Prompts (as useful)

- What forms of repeated stress are implied, and how are they registered indirectly?
- How does the poem move between flexibility and rigidity without privileging either?
- Where does damage appear as a condition for reinforcement?
- How does the poem handle time—through duration, accumulation, or event?
- What changes if the final naming is removed? What changes if it appears earlier?

Pressure

- The poem may be approached by observing how pressure accumulates through repeated impact rather than singular force.
- The ending can be treated as an outcome of endurance rather than resolution.

Optional Compositional Extension

- A related exercise might involve tracing the effects of repeated stress on a material or body.
- Allow transformation to appear as a byproduct rather than a goal.
- The poem may stop where adaptation becomes visible.

Callus

A thousand heel strikes:
skips,
jumps—

a flexible bow,
stiff—
a fractured bone—

callus.

Structural Use (Optional) — Road Rash

Possible Entry
One way into the poem is to attend to how abrupt shifts in balance produce consequence without preparation.

Discussion Prompts (as useful)

- What moments of control or momentum are implied before disruption occurs?
- How does the poem register impact indirectly rather than descriptively?
- Where does effort reappear after the initial loss of balance?
- How do directional terms (left, up, down) organize the poem's movement?
- What changes if the final naming is removed? What changes if it is anticipated earlier?

Pressure

- The poem may be approached by observing how pressure is released through sudden interruption rather than gradual buildup.
- The ending can be treated as an aftereffect rather than a resolution.

Optional Compositional Extension

- A related exercise might involve tracing the immediate aftermath of a sudden physical shift.
- Allow consequence to appear without narrative explanation.
- The poem may stop where momentum gives way to residue.

Road Rash

Sudden left lean—
shoved by the asphalt,
a straight run.

Upslope,
downshift—
a cramped leg—

hot fatty tissue.

Structural Use (Optional) — White Smoke

Possible Entry
One way into the poem is to attend to how a series of careful actions gives way to dispersal and residue.

Discussion Prompts (as useful)

- What forms of preparation or precision appear early, and how are they marked materially?
- How does the poem move from containment toward release without narrative explanation?
- Where do acts of sealing or closure occur, and how are they later undone?
- How do gaps or ellipses function in the poem's progression?
- What changes if the final image is removed? What changes if the sequence ends earlier?

Pressure

- The poem may be approached by observing how pressure is generated through accumulation and then allowed to dissipate.
- The ending can be treated as dispersal rather than resolution.

Optional Compositional Extension

- A related exercise might involve tracing a sequence of careful actions that culminates in residue or loss.
- Allow objects to shift from utility to aftermath.
- The poem may stop where material presence thins into trace.

White Smoke

Walnut escritoire,
faded green felt,
a well of ink—
pounce.

Dib a nib—
fluttering goose quill:
a pink kiss—
a red seal.

. . .

Broken wax,
a jug of wine—
tipped,
hollow.

A flickering wick—
an ember—
white smoke.

Structural Use (Optional) — Tessellation

Possible Entry
One way into the poem is to attend to how repetition produces pattern without stabilizing form.

Discussion Prompts (as useful)

- What kinds of units are repeated, and how do they vary as they accumulate?
- How does the poem handle growth through adjacency rather than expansion?
- Where does nesting give way to crowding or distortion?
- How do shifts in shape or texture register without narrative framing?
- What changes if the final compression is removed? What changes if repetition is reduced?

Pressure

- The poem may be approached by observing how pressure intensifies through unchecked accumulation.
- The ending can be treated as a density point rather than a conclusion.

Optional Compositional Extension

- A related exercise might involve repeating a single form while allowing its boundaries to degrade or blur.
- Allow pattern to emerge through piling rather than order.
- The poem may stop where accumulation becomes unstable.

Tessellation

A stack of daughters—
circular,
elongated—

nesting…
heaping…

A lump—
frayed—

heaping…

Structural Use (Optional) — Tavy

Possible Entry

One way into the poem is to attend to how proximity and relation are established through naming rather than explanation.

Discussion Prompts (as useful)

- What kinds of connections are implied between the elements named, and how are they held without description?
- How does the poem rely on suggestion rather than sequence?
- Where does scale shift—from intimate contact to abundance?
- How does the final naming function in relation to what precedes it?
- What changes if the central pairing is removed? What changes if the ending is withheld?

Pressure

- The poem may be approached by observing how pressure is generated through associative placement rather than accumulation.
- The ending can be treated as a point of orientation rather than a resolution.

Optional Compositional Extension

- A related exercise might involve placing paired images in close proximity without clarifying their relationship.
- Allow naming to function as connection rather than explanation.
- The poem may stop where association holds.

Tavy

Deep nectaries—
flickering moth tongue.

Wild custard apples
dangling,
comet orchids.

Structural Use (Optional) — Infinity

Possible Entry
One way into the poem is to attend to how vastness is reduced through containment rather than negation.

Discussion Prompts (as useful)

- What forms of enclosure or framing appear, and how do they limit what they hold?
- How does the poem move from abstraction toward object or vessel?
- Where does sound or smoke function as a stand-in for what cannot be held?
- How does scale shift across the poem without transition?
- What changes if the final silence is removed? What changes if it appears earlier?

Pressure

- The poem may be approached by observing how pressure is generated through compression of magnitude.
- The ending can be treated as cessation rather than closure.

Optional Compositional Extension

- A related exercise might involve placing an abstract concept inside a series of concrete containers.
- Allow reduction to occur without explanation.
- The poem may stop where containment gives way to quiet.

Infinity

Infinity…
shrunk to a statue—
a Dorian chant,
smoke,

contained in a book,
a cup,
veil.

Silence.

Structural Use (Optional) — Qualia

Possible Entry
One way into the poem is to attend to how internal experience is rendered through material or mechanical imagery.

Discussion Prompts (as useful)

- What forms of mediation appear between thought and sensation?
- How does the poem juxtapose abstraction with everyday sensory detail?
- Where does the language suggest repetition or reproduction rather than originality?
- How do the sensory elements function without being elaborated?
- What changes if the final naming is removed? What changes if it appears earlier?

Pressure

- The poem may be approached by observing how pressure arises from the gap between experience and description.
- The ending can be treated as a label rather than an explanation.

Optional Compositional Extension

- A related exercise might involve pairing an internal state with an external, mechanical image.
- Allow sensation to appear without interpretation.
- The poem may stop where naming replaces articulation.

Qualia

Thoughts—
stapled to a neuron,
photocopy dreams—

bitter coffee,
grief.

Structural Use (Optional) — Chilling Hour

Possible Entry
One way into the poem is to attend to how heat and damage coexist with conditions for emergence.

Discussion Prompts (as useful)

- What forms of burning or decay appear, and how are they registered sensorially?
- How does the poem place moments of ignition beside moments of cracking or opening?
- Where does atmosphere function as evidence rather than setting?
- How does the shift from damage to emergence occur without transition?
- What changes if the final naming is removed? What changes if the central moment is withheld?

Pressure

- The poem may be approached by observing how pressure is sustained through simultaneous destruction and potential.
- The ending can be treated as ignition rather than resolution.

Optional Compositional Extension

- A related exercise might involve placing an image of damage beside an image of emergence.
- Allow heat or light to function as catalyst without explanation.
- The poem may stop where transformation becomes possible but incomplete.

Chilling Hour

Alligator charring,
ghost logs—
sickly-sweet air.

Chilling hour,
red light flash,
a seed cracks—

Ember Rose.

Structural Use (Optional) — Gazpacho

Possible Entry
One way into the poem is to attend to how containment preserves contradiction rather than resolving it.

Discussion Prompts (as useful)

- What opposing conditions are held together within the same vessel?
- How does the poem emphasize separation through layers, walls, or narrowing?
- Where does insulation function as both protection and isolation?
- How does light operate as a limited intrusion rather than illumination?
- What changes if the final naming is removed? What changes if the container is described less precisely?

Pressure

- The poem may be approached by observing how pressure is sustained through enclosure and restriction.
- The ending can be treated as a seal rather than a conclusion.

Optional Compositional Extension

- A related exercise might involve placing incompatible states inside a single container.
- Allow structure or vessel to do the work of holding tension.
- The poem may stop where containment remains intact.

Gazpacho

Steamy soup in a vacuum—
double glass walls.

A narrow neck—
corked,
light seepage—

III. Echoes

Structural Use (Optional) — Sponge Cycle

Possible Entry
One way into the poem is to attend to how material changes state through repeated exposure and pressure.

Discussion Prompts (as useful)

- What stages of transformation are suggested, and how are they marked materially?
- How does the poem handle saturation versus compression?
- Where does motion give way to weight or density?
- How do color and texture function as indicators of change?
- What changes if the final condition is removed? What changes if the cycle does not repeat?

Pressure

- The poem may be approached by observing how pressure accumulates through absorption and release.
- The ending can be treated as a fixed state rather than a conclusion.

Optional Compositional Extension

- A related exercise might involve tracing a single object through multiple material states.
- Allow transformation to occur through environment rather than intention.
- The poem may stop where change hardens into form.

Residue

Brittle—
purple and porous,
dangling from a dish,
dropped in a deluge.

Swollen pulp,
plants—
pressed, plowed—
shimmering quartz counter.

Drooped in a dish,
purple and pitted—

petrified.

Structural Use (Optional) — Ghost Perch

Possible Entry
One way into the poem is to attend to how readiness and suspension are held without action.

Discussion Prompts (as useful)

- What kinds of presence are suggested through stillness rather than movement?
- How do sound and silence interact across the images?
- Where does potential action remain unfulfilled?
- How do predator and proximity function without contact?
- What changes if the final naming is removed? What changes if motion is introduced?

Pressure

- The poem may be approached by observing how pressure is sustained through poised imbalance.
- The ending can be treated as continued suspension rather than resolution.

Optional Compositional Extension

- A related exercise might involve placing multiple agents in proximity without allowing interaction.
- Allow tension to arise from readiness rather than event.
- The poem may stop where stillness holds.

Ghost Perch

Owl on a limb—
poised.

A buzzing bat,
silent hornet—

ghost perch.

Structural Use (Optional) — Koala Plate

Possible Entry
One way into the poem is to attend to how context determines function rather than substance.

Discussion Prompts (as useful)

- What conditions appear necessary for recognition or engagement?
- How does the poem place an object inside an environment that alters its usability?
- Where does need or deprivation register without explanation?
- How do surface and setting function differently across the images?
- What changes if the environmental context is removed? What changes if the object remains but its support shifts?

Pressure

- The poem may be approached by observing how pressure arises from misalignment between capacity and condition.
- The ending can be treated as a stalled state rather than a conclusion.

Optional Compositional Extension

- A related exercise might involve presenting a necessary object in an unusable context.
- Allow constraint to emerge from placement rather than refusal.
- The poem may stop where recognition fails to occur.

Koala Plate

Eucalyptus.
A flat plate.

Koala eyes—
sunken.

Structural Use (Optional) — Chef's Kiss

Possible Entry
One way into the poem is to attend to how a sequence of tactile actions leads toward a moment of completion.

Discussion Prompts (as useful)

- What kinds of manual processes are foregrounded, and how are they paced?
- How does the poem move from preparation to assembly without narrating intention?
- Where do sound and texture function as indicators of progress?
- How does containment (pot, crust) shape the movement toward finishing?
- What changes if the final gesture is removed? What changes if it appears earlier?

Pressure

- The poem may be approached by observing how pressure accumulates through incremental refinement.
- The ending can be treated as a closure of process rather than a culmination of meaning.

Optional Compositional Extension

- A related exercise might involve tracing a series of physical actions that culminate in a single, minimal gesture.
- Allow satisfaction to register without commentary.
- The poem may stop where process seals itself.

Chef's Kiss

Cranked—
cracked seeds,
a slopping blade.

Strained pulp
gurgling—
steaming terracotta
pot.

Ricotta on top—
green leaf—
a crust of bread.

Structural Use (Optional) — Gaze

Possible Entry
One way into the poem is to attend to how signals accumulate without leading to execution.

Discussion Prompts (as useful)

- What forms of communication are presented, and how are they separated from outcome?
- How does the poem build expectation through gesture rather than action?
- Where does repetition function as suspension rather than confirmation?
- How do pauses and ellipses contribute to delay?
- What changes if the final return is removed? What changes if an action follows?

Pressure

- The poem may be approached by observing how pressure is generated through anticipation without release.
- The ending can be treated as a reset rather than a conclusion.

Optional Compositional Extension

- A related exercise might involve presenting a sequence of cues that never result in action.
- Allow meaning to reside in preparation rather than event.
- The poem may stop where expectation remains unresolved.

Gaze

Gaze…

One finger—
heater…

a wiggle—
a change-up…

fist—
high and tight…

Gaze…

Structural Use (Optional) — Antiseptic

Possible Entry
One way into the poem is to attend to how damage and intervention are placed in direct sequence without commentary.

Discussion Prompts (as useful)

- What forms of injury or contamination appear, and how are they registered materially?
- How does the poem move from uncontrolled damage toward deliberate incision?
- Where does precision replace excess, and what is lost in the process?
- How do sensory cues (color, temperature, breath) function across the sequence?
- What changes if the final image is removed? What changes if cleanliness is introduced earlier?

Pressure

- The poem may be approached by observing how pressure intensifies through necessity rather than choice.
- The ending can be treated as a residual state rather than resolution.

Optional Compositional Extension

- A related exercise might involve tracing a progression from damage to intervention using only physical detail.
- Allow cleanliness or relief to appear without explanation or moral framing.
- The poem may stop where control is restored but consequence remains.

Antiseptic

Broken leg—
green-black slime—
truncated.

A stone—
a blind incision—
surgical fever.

Clean cuts—
shimmering floorboards—

mint breath.

Structural Use (Optional) — Epoxy

Possible Entry
One way into the poem is to attend to how attachment and removal operate as physical processes rather than symbolic acts.

Discussion Prompts (as useful)

- What kinds of adhesion or fixing are suggested, and where do they resist easy separation?
- How does the poem move between motion and stasis without resolving either?
- Where does intervention occur, and how is it marked materially?
- How do surface treatments (buffed, matte, shimmering) function as records of action?
- What changes if the final recontextualized image is removed? What changes if the act of prying is omitted?

Pressure

- The poem may be approached by observing how pressure accumulates through attachment and is redistributed through removal.
- The ending can be treated as re-siting rather than resolution.

Optional Compositional Extension

- A related exercise might involve tracing the life of an object as it is fixed, removed, and repurposed.
- Allow residue and surface alteration to carry the effects of action.
- The poem may stop where adhesion gives way to placement.

Epoxy

She dances with a pothole,
sings to a speed bump,
glued to the dash—
epoxy.

I pry her with a putty,
tuck her in the glove—
buff smooth,
matte—
shimmering vinyl
spot.

Sun through glass,
a pale shadow—
flower pedestal
in the glare.

Structural Use (Optional) — Panhandle Hook

Possible Entry
One way into the poem is to attend to how force registers through fracture and absence rather than sustained motion.

Discussion Prompts (as useful)

- What kinds of pressure or compression are implied before rupture occurs?
- How does the poem handle moments of breakage without narrating cause?
- Where does sound appear, and how quickly does it give way to silence?
- How do environmental forms persist after the event that shaped them?
- What changes if the moment of fracture is removed? What changes if silence is delayed?

Pressure

- The poem may be approached by observing how pressure is released through sudden break and then redistributed across the landscape.
- The ending can be treated as residual shaping rather than resolution.

Optional Compositional Extension

- A related exercise might involve tracing the aftermath of a force through what remains rather than what occurs.
- Allow form to appear as evidence of prior action.
- The poem may stop where motion has passed but structure endures.

Panhandle Hook

Panhandle hook,
packed over frost.

Cracked slab—
a tree snaps—
plume.

Jagged air,
silence—

wind sculpted ridges.

Structural Use (Optional) — Box Jelly

Possible Entry
One way into the poem is to attend to how perception and response occur without deliberation.

Discussion Prompts (as useful)

- What forms of awareness are suggested, and how are they rendered as partial or diffuse?
- How does the poem place visibility alongside concealment?
- Where does scale fluctuate between diminishment and inflation?
- How do proximity and danger emerge without narrative buildup?
- What changes if the final action is removed? What changes if it occurs earlier?

Pressure

- The poem may be approached by observing how pressure arises from misalignment between perception and consequence.
- The ending can be treated as an event without intention rather than a resolution.

Optional Compositional Extension

- A related exercise might involve presenting an entity that reacts without cognition.
- Allow threat to emerge from structure rather than motive.
- The poem may stop where contact replaces awareness.

Box Jelly

Brainless box jelly
hidden in light.

Eye clusters—
out of focus—
a mangrove.

Inflated body—
a fake giant—

sting.

Structural Use (Optional) — Tennis Court

Possible Entry
One way into the poem is to attend to how acts of measurement attempt precision while continually shifting scale.

Discussion Prompts (as useful)

- What different kinds of measurement are presented, and how do they differ in method or intimacy?
- How does the poem move from external objects toward internal space?
- Where does scale expand unexpectedly, and where does it contract?
- How does repetition of measuring gestures function without establishing control?
- What changes if the final comparison is removed? What changes if it appears earlier?

Pressure

- The poem may be approached by observing how pressure arises from the mismatch between tools and what they attempt to measure.
- The ending can be treated as a disproportion rather than a conclusion.

Optional Compositional Extension

- A related exercise might involve applying precise measuring language to increasingly incongruent objects or spaces.
- Allow scale to shift without justification.
- The poem may stop where comparison overwhelms accuracy.

Tennis Court

I measure a bag
with a tape,

an airway
with a scan,

a sac,
with a scope—

a small lung—
a tennis court.

Afterword

Pressure does not resolve. It transfers.

When force moves through a system, something remains: a deformation, a residue, a record of contact. What you have read are not conclusions, but traces—marks left by matter, language, and attention after stress has passed through.

Nothing here is meant to be remembered whole. The poems function independently, like surfaces subjected to different loads. Some hold. Some fail. Some appear unchanged.

That appearance is unreliable.

These pieces do not build toward meaning. They register conditions. They stop where further motion would require explanation or release. What remains is not an answer, but a state.

The system ends here.
The pressure does not.

Acknowledgments

This book was shaped by constraints rather than collaboration. Still, no system forms in isolation.

Thanks to those who applied pressure—through resistance, silence, procedure, or refusal—and in doing so clarified limits rather than smoothing them over. Thanks to the materials, tools, and conditions that failed honestly and left records of that failure.

Any remaining faults belong to the author.

Appendix

Paradox Structure

Each poem in this collection arises from a three-part pressure system:

- Polarity A
- Polarity B
- Liminal State

These are not themes or oppositions to be resolved. They are conditions held in tension. The poem forms within that field and stops where pressure remains active.

Not all three elements are equally visible. In some poems, one polarity dominates. In others, the liminal state is all that remains.

Expressive Thirds

Many poems move through three expressive registers:

- Matter — physical processes, materials, forces
- Mind — cognition, measurement, attention, intervention

- Being — existence under pressure, after contact, or at limit

This movement may be linear, compressed, inverted, or partial. Some poems never leave the material register. Others collapse rapidly from matter into being. The structure is descriptive, not prescriptive.

Orbits of Compression

Poems operate at different distances from their central pressure point:

- First orbit — Direct. Images are accessible; tension is legible.
- Second orbit — Liminal. The pressure is active but partially withheld.
- Third orbit — Compressed. Language is dense; reference is minimal.

Greater distance requires more sustained attention. This is intentional.

Scientific Language

All terminology used in this book is literal. Many terms are ecological, geological, anatomical, mechanical, or physical. Nothing is invented for metaphorical effect.

If a word feels unfamiliar, the friction is part of the reading experience. The language does not symbolize the process. It names it.

Examples include, but are not limited to:

- Step leaders
- Pillow lava
- Hayflick limit
- Nurse logs
- Box jellyfish
- Coastline paradox
- Delayed-choice quantum erasure

Nothing is symbolic unless the reader decides to treat it as such.

On Interpretation

Interpretation is not prohibited. It is deferred.

These poems are not puzzles to be solved but systems to be observed. They do not yield meaning through explanation. They respond to pressure.

If a poem appears to resist interpretation, that resistance is part of its structure. Pressing harder may produce insight—or deformation.

Both are valid outcomes.

About the Author

J. A. Gucci writes poems that operate as systems rather than narratives. His work draws from ecological, anatomical, mechanical, and physical processes, favoring compression, constraint, and structural pressure over metaphor or confession.

He is interested in how language behaves under stress, how attention alters systems, and how form can register contact without explanation. His poems resist symbolism, minimize speaker presence, and privilege observation over interpretation.

He lives and works in the United States.

Colophon

This book was set in a serif typeface chosen for clarity under compression and printed on acid-free paper. It was designed as a closed system, with attention to spacing, lineation, and page tension.

The manuscript was assembled and revised in stages, with emphasis on constraint, sequencing, and structural integrity. All poems were written by the author.

Printed in the United States.

www.ingramcontent.com/pod-product-compliance
Lightning Source LLC
LaVergne TN
LVHW041605070526
838199LV00052B/2990